Rebuilding the Polymath

And Other Insights into the World of Innovation

Steve Spalding
and
James Gibson

Copyright © 2013
Innovate GSB LLC
All rights reserved.

ISBN: 978-1-300-73783-4

Author's Notes

I. Before you begin reading, know this: this is not a academic text, or even a popular science book. It is a manifesto. We use contractions, because that is how we speak. We don't cite sources in line because footnotes detract from preaching. That said, we hope you enjoy our work. – James Gibson

II. When I was doing the final edit, I was just about to leave note I out, it's a wee self-conscious for my tastes, but James likes it and I trust James when it comes to the academic stuff. That being said, what I think you should know is that this Manifesto is best read with a cup of coffee – light creamer, two sugars. Alternatively, with one sugar and an open mind. – Steve Spalding

A Rallying Cry

The challenges of today can be solved. Solved by clever men and women willing to look them in the eye and apply their talents to solving them. This is our rallying call -- that the world can be improved, that excellence is a process, and that the spirit of innovation can and should be supported and encouraged.

Just look at the untapped potential in today's world, the thousands of tinkerers and creators who are not pursuing their ideas for reasons that, as we will explain, are wholly surmountable. We want to undam this river and release a torrent of productive innovation that will change the lives of every human for the better.

Now let's begin.

Part 1
An Amazing World

The world is amazing.

Since the 1950s, science and industry has brought us the jet airplane, space travel, computers, smartphones, the human genome project, the Internet and a seemingly endless parade of other innovations that have reshaped the way we live.

Many of these developments required massive, coordinated efforts. The Apollo moon missions alone employed some 400,000 people across 20,000 firms and organizations. While most were engaged in manufacturing components, many more were doing the design, engineering and basic scientific research necessary to bring us to the Moon. Many of these scientists and engineers devoted much of their lives to specializing in narrow fields in physics, chemistry, materials science, and engineering in order to gain the expertise they needed to make this happen.

This is to be expected. As science has progressed and systems have grown increasingly complex, more and more knowledge is required to work anywhere near the cutting edge. New developments in hard problems require vast efforts simply because we already know so much. As evidence, consider that today the average published scientific paper has 3.5 authors, while in 1960 it had just 1.9. This corresponds to ½ of all papers being published by individuals in 1960 to more than ½ needing more than 3 authors today.

This specialization extends to education. Why get a PhD in finance when one can just as easily specialize in *mathematical* finance, *computational* finance, *statistical* finance, *behavioral* finance, or a laundry list of even deeper specializations, each with its own distinct program?

This is not necessarily a bad thing. While the faceless machine of Big Science does not inspire children with the kind of fairy-book zeal that stories of apples falling on Newton's head can, it does its job. Science gets done, and new knowledge is generated for the benefit of all. All of this specialization can, however, begin to remind us of the saying that one can "know more and more about less and less until you know everything about nothing".

Big Science, Big Industry

As in science, in industry. New products and inventions require much the same level of effort to launch. While it is still possible for individuals and small groups to design and create novel devices, they are often limited in scope and have trouble competing with more established corporate efforts.

During World War II, a team of engineers at North American Aviation took the P-51 Mustang from specifications on a contract to a flying prototype in just 102 days. Most of the engineers had only bachelor's degrees, and they worked without the aid of electronic computers. Today, the most advanced fighter aircraft in the world is Lockheed Martin's F-22 Raptor, which first flew on 7 September 1997 - some 16 years after the initial specification was published. Many, if not most of the engineers who worked on the F-22 had Master's degrees or PhD's.

Design complexity is not limited to stealthy interceptors flying twice the speed of sound. One of the most successful products on the crowd-funding site KickStarter is the Pebble Watch, an e-ink, programmable smart watch. While Pebble's excellent team of 5 is more than capable of creating a smart watch with the backing of 85,000 preorders and several million dollars, the many delays the project has suffered through in design and manufacturing begins to show us some of the major limitations small producers face.

Apple's iPhone, the device that brought smartphones into the public consciousness, provides a prime example of the power of big industry. Apple has over 72,000 employees, a far cry from the dusty garage where the original Apple I computer was developed by Jobs and Woz. When you compare these 72,000 manufacturers, designers, engineers, analysts and marketers against Pebble's 5 visionaries, the cause of Pebble's delays becomes clear. It is simply impossible for such a small team to have the supply chain, logistical support, technical design staff, and basic manufacturing capability that a behemoth like Apple can muster. The result is that the Pebbles of the world will tend to disappoint mainstream consumers, not because the products themselves are inferior but because today we expect so much more than in the days of the P-51.

This is not to say that the world is entirely bereft of lone inventors and small scale innovators, rather it's that these men and women are often limited in what they can hope to accomplish: while a dorm room start up can lead to the next Facebook, these same tinkerers will have a much harder time developing broad market consumer hardware, or say running experiments in high energy Physics.

Building on the Web

But what about the web? Even though many web projects require a significant initial investment and are highly complex, the start-up costs are far lower than in other industries. While launching a Subway sandwich shop to serve a hundred customers per day might cost a hundred thousand dollars, launching a website to serve ten thousand customers might only be a few bucks a month and a few hundred hours of coding.

Our most successful Internet stalwarts often started on these shoestring budgets. Facebook began as a project that Mark Zuckerberg pursued in his free time at Harvard College; although it later took millions in Venture Capital and still occasionally struggles with profitability, the initial investment on Zuckerberg's part was no more than a few thousand dollars - an amount even an impoverished student can assemble, given reason to.

Google developed from the PhD dissertation of its founders, Larry Paige and Sergei Brin. The initial investment required to launch the service was high by web standards, as the project aimed to index the entire web, but compared to launching our sandwich shop, the investment was still miniscule. The highest cost faced by a newly minted Google was acquiring enough hardware to do the indexing: fortunately, as grad students at Stanford University, Brin and Page had the luxury of being able to piggy back on University infrastructure to accomplish that task.

These are just the most famous examples, but others abound.

Groupon, Pandora, Reddit, (the defunct and now relaunched) MySpace, Air BnB, and many other companies all started from humble beginnings, and were able to expand chiefly because of the web's zero-marginal-cost development model.

In this light, the web must be seen as the great democratizer, anybody who has the ability to view a website has the hardware to create a website. And almost anyone with the drive and motivation to read one of the thousands of "how-to program" tutorials dotting the web can learn the skills necessary to build a commercial product.

So there's our answer right? Sure we need specialists to build iPhones but who really cares? The Internet has given everyone the ability to create whatever else their imaginations and their credit limits will allow. We are on the cusp of a brave new world, a world where we are all artists, and the web is our canvas.

Perhaps. But it certainly doesn't feel that way, does it?

Maybe it's because we so often forget that the web is only one, small piece of the landscape. While it and it's power to fast track innovation is easy to point to, we must remember that we live in a world of atoms as much as a world of bits, and for the last half century those atoms have increasingly become the realm of Big Industry, and researching those atoms, increasingly the realm of Big Science. The question we want to ask then is whether this was always the case - that most new products required vast armies of highly specialized scientists and engineers? That one needed more more than a decade of education just to begin to grasp some tiny field of knowledge?

The answer we've arrived at is no.

Remembering the Polymath

Think of an inventor, businessman, or scientist who lived before the second World War. Sir Isaac Newton, Benjamin Franklin, Thomas Edison, or a dozen others besides probably comes to mind. While these men had nearly nothing in common, one thing did bind them together, none were constrained by the kinds of intellectual specialization that rule the world today.

Isaac Newton is well known for his early development of a theory of gravity, but should also be remembered for creating Calculus (though its providence is under some contention), contributions to optics, his work in the study of thermodynamics, along with many innovations in astronomy and mathematics. All of this is in addition to being a member of parliament and the head of the Royal Mint.

In Newton's time there were only a handful of universities, almost all sponsored by the church. They placed equal emphasis on theology, classic Greek and Latin texts, and mathematics. At Cambridge, Newton's alma mater, degrees were awarded on the basis of extensive oral examinations and completing a bachelor's degree could easily take seven years. What this education lacked in depth, it made up for by exposing students to most of the important subjects of the age – including an extensive *scientific* curriculum.

Although "science" as a subject was not taught at universities in Newton's time, its equivalent - natural philosophy - was popular. While natural philosophy was often conflated with pseudo-sciences like alchemy in the late 1600s, it did represent a real step forward in the empirical investigation of the natural world. It also drove the creation of new organizations like The Royal Society of London for Improving Natural Knowledge, which brought these early scientists together with the mission of expanding the frontiers of human thought. Appropriately, Newton was one of the society's earliest members.

Since academia was so small, there were no hard and fast divisions of Major to discourage the study of divergent fields: Newton would not have hesitated to study optics or biology or astronomy, as all of these fields were part of the same pursuit of knowledge that natural philosophy represented.

By Franklin's time a century later there was more knowledge, but not so much that a well read and clever man could not learn most of it. Franklin was such a man, and is remembered as much for his experiments on natural phenomena as he is for his inventions - bifocals, the Franklin stove, and the lightning rod among others. He also served as a statesman, helping found a precursor to the US Postal Service, as well as working as an ambassador for the new United States to France.

Though none of his scientific accomplishments are as well regarded as Newton's *Principia*, he was able to make inroads in fields that Newton never touched: in 1780, for example, Franklin spent his days negotiating France's support for the rebelling English colony he now called his home, while at night he conducted some of the first experiments on electricity. Though certainly eccentric, no gentleman of the era would think it improper for one man to serve in such a wide variety of roles.

While the Royal Society and old universities like Oxford and Cambridge began expanding their curriculum to include topics in natural sciences, Franklin went one step further. The University of Pennsylvania, one of the world's top universities, was founded with Franklin's aid: his mission was not simply to create another seminary (as Harvard was originally founded) but to create an institution that also taught the practical skills required for business and public service. It is not hard to infer that Franklin wanted more men to imitate him and his diverse range of accomplishments.

Later still we have the example of Thomas Edison. While Edison was chiefly an inventor, he was also massively successful in business. Remarkably, he received 1093 patents in the United States alone, an accomplishment not matched until the 1980s. He is most famous for patenting practical versions of the electric light bulb, but was also awarded patents for many other electrical devices, including telegraph and telephone systems, electrical generators, stock tickers, and many more.

Although several were simple improvements on previous work, a few were unprecedented, including the phonograph and fluoroscope. It was his ability to transform these inventions into practical businesses, however, that really separated Edison from his contemporaries. While today we are quick to point to the rivalry between Tesla and Edison - casting Edison in the role of greedy businessman to Tesla's honest selflessness, one must respect the diversity of skills required for Edison to so successfully pursue research and business simultaneously. While Tesla died in poverty, Edison founded 14 companies - among which was General Electric, today one of the largest companies in the world.

Forgetting Again

Now, think of a famous modern scientist. If you are a scientist yourself, you may have latched onto someone in your own field. It is unlikely though that Martinus Veltman, Ahmed Zewali, or Gunter Blobel came to mind. Who are these men? They are the 1999 Nobel Prize winners in Physics, Chemistry, and Medicine, arguably some of the world's top thinkers.

If you are not a scientist, you might have thought of Niel DeGrass Tyson or Stephen Hawking, two famous contemporary physicists. Both of these men are incredibly accomplished and very well known, however, even they do not have recognition in the variety of fields that marked their prewar cousins.

None of the great polymaths - Newton, Franklin, Edison - exist today, but not because of some change in genetics that decreased the number of savants born. Part of the answer is that there *is* simply more knowledge. Newton could learn much of the math that there was to know by reading Euclid. Although there was more to know by Franklin's time, the edifice of knowledge was not so vast as to be insurmountable. For Edison's part, we must recall that most of his work focused on electrical devices. Today many of these "easy" innovations have already been found, and what we are left with requires more and more specialized information to grasp. Clearly then, the massive increase in human knowledge that marked the modern era contributes to the problem, but we don't believe it's the only part of the story.

We theorize that the most important change, the one that has brought us to our world of hyper-specialization, occurred during World War II. The Manhattan Project, launched by the US Government in order to create an Atomic Bomb, was one of the biggest hard science projects ever conceived. It required hundreds of man-years of effort from thousands of scientists and a legion of supporting technicians. As one of the hardest scientific challenges ever faced by mankind, it necessitated an entirely new level of organization and specialization.

The Manhattan Project's success was partially responsible for the rise of Big Science and Big Industry after the war. With the shining example of what a massive, coordinate research effort could accomplish, the United States entered the postwar era looking for problems to apply their new-found systems to. There were plenty available. In particular, the Cold War Space Race provided a perfect opportunity for the application of vast resources to hard, creative projects.

Of course, when one holds a hammer, everything can start to look like a nail. Between the continuous Communist scares and the almost religious zeal to "beat the soviets" in space, the United States and the western world mobilized to create more raw material for the machine of Big Science. School programs at all levels were re-worked to place new emphasis on mathematics and science, but these changes were not geared toward create new Edisons, Newtons, or Franklins. Instead, the reforms were designed and succeeded at creating thousands of highly specialized cogs for the hungry machines of Big Science and Big Industry.

These changes had, and continue to have value. Many problems can't be solved by a lone inventor working in a lab, and require the dedicated, organized, and systematic application of the efforts of thousands. What we lament is the change in culture - the paradigm of specialization that pervades the world today. While we need the machinery of Big Science and the specialists that make it possible, we also need the creative polymaths, men and women not bound by labels on degrees and job descriptions. This Manifesto is about how we can bring them back.

Part 2
Three Excuses

I wish.

I wish I had enough money to take the time.
I wish I had enough time to devote the energy.
I wish I had the right skills to make it real.

If I did I could, if I did I could, if only I did I could...

This has become the klaxon call of an entire class of modern entrepreneurials. They have the drive, they have the hunger but at least within the confines of their own minds they lack the resources, the skills, and the confidence that would give them the right to be great.

These barriers pile up and time ticks on and responsibilities replace desire with need until many of these people, people who might have otherwise made a real go at building out their dreams, are left with nothing more productive than dozens of pages of notes and dozens more aborted projects.

At best what we see here is an inefficient use of talent, at worst it's a dangerous and tragic loss of potential innovation.

What we don't see are simple excuses, hand-wringing justifying stasis. Instead, these pleas are symptoms, symptoms of a system that has existed at least since the second World War that has increasingly shifted the ideal of the innovator away from the free wheeling, broad-minded "universal man" of the Renaissance towards the focused and disciplined bench scientist of the 1950s. It's a system that has regimented creativity and society alongside it. In doing so, it has brought us the entire edifice on which modern technological progress is built, but it has also stolen from us a template.

The Template of the Polymath

From Leibniz and Newton to Pascal and Franklin, polymaths were innovators who used their time and talents to pursue a broad range of social and scientific pursuits. Newton, for example, was a physicist, mathematician, astronomer, theologian, natural philosopher and alchemist. Benjamin Franklin was an author, political theorist, politician, printer, scientist, inventor, and diplomat. All of these people devoted their efforts to the exploration of knowledge itself, and through these varied pursuits were able to develop some of the most important discoveries of our time.

The modern system of forty hour work weeks, hyper-specialized degrees, Big Science, Big Industry and rising financial dependence has left our society with little room for these "shiftless generalists," men and women without the discipline to pursue a single subject to its finest detail, or the desire to define in business plan or SWOT analysis where they hope their pursuits will lead. Even in the realm of entrepreneurship, a realm where you'd imagine this lost class would thrive, we have made a virtue of focus and specificity to the exclusion of discovery and adaptation, which has left us hard pressed to find anyone with the will and the ability to integrate differing disciplines of knowledge into new invention, as the Wright Brothers used their knowledge of bicycle design to build airplanes and Leonardo Di Vinci transformed his powers of observation and attention to detail into a range of artistic and technological innovations.

How does this system work? How has society undermined this

class of creators? Let's take a look at each aspect of the complaint to see.

The Money Trap

Historically innovation has been the domain of those who, whether by patronage or independent wealth, were provided with the comfortable certainty that they would be able to feed themselves and their family. The money itself was not the key though, instead our focus should be how it was used and how those uses differ from our relationship with money today.

The Medici of the Renaissance are probably our most famous example of patrons. A group of powerful, wealthy and politically connected bankers, the Medici used their wealth to fund grand artistic projects, from the reconstruction of the church of San Lorenzo and the monastery of San Marco under Cosimo di Medici, to funding great artists like Donatello and architects like Michelozzo di Bartolommeo. For them wealth was not an end in itself, but a means to a greater goal, be it influence, political authority or simple public relations. For those who found themselves supported by Medici patronage, money was fuel, fuel that allowed them the time, freedom and credibility to build great works that would have otherwise been too elaborate, too expensive or too time intensive to create on their own. The Medici maintained these artist's lifestyles, providing them with places to stay, food to eat and a means to create. In exchange, these artists provided the Medici with great works that they could take credit for and use to further their social agenda.

Compare this to our modern concept of wealth, where money is a tool used for two major purposes, the first is to support a lifestyle -- to pay a mortgage, purchase food, buy health insurance and pay for a car. The second is as a means to increase comfort through the purchase of commodities. Under this regime, any money beyond what we need to support ourselves and maintain the health and safety of our families is to be used towards the purchase of more "things," things we believe will ultimately make us content. The dream of wealth then is the dream of unlimited access to stuff, and the pursuit of wealth is couched in the language of commodity. We want to be able to afford that fancy car, the new boat, the bigger house, the elegant clothes, and the expensive dinners, not because these will make us happier in any lasting way (years of research has proven that they won't) but because they will prove to the world and to ourselves that we have succeeded at living.

We can see this by looking at the national savings rate, which hovers at around 4%. To put this in perspective, according to the Bureau of Labor Statistics, the median American made $51,260 in 2010. Given this rate of savings, this person only managed to put away $2,048 a year. Assume about 75% of that ($1,536) went into a tax advantaged retirement account which made our friend a generous 6% annually. In that case, after 30 years of savings he would be left with $128,719.

Unfortunately, by most estimates, at retirement he will have about 19 more years to live, and at an average of $26,567 of expenses per year (excluding taxes), only about 5 years of savings to live on. Behavioral economists call this "buy now, pay later" mentality hyperbolic discounting and it's something we are becoming increasingly good at, selling our future comfort away to the present for pennies on the dollar.

Add to this the debt that we use to support our "stuff" habits and the image becomes even more clear, the average American carries around about $7,200 worth of revolving credit debt. This average, however, is a bit misleading because there is a significant portion of the population with limited to nonexistent revolving debt. For those with debt then, the amount of debt they hold can be many times this number, and this doesn't begin to include the mortgages and student loans which make up a huge portion of the debt load for many families. The end result is that many households can't even afford the rather modest savings rate we described earlier, partially because so much more money is going towards consumption rather than towards savings and investing.

The ultimate result is that we are a nation made up almost entirely of consumers rather than investors, we don't produce a great number of Medici's because even among our high income earners, a large portion of their wealth and debt go towards the consumption of goods rather than the direct production of great works (there are notable exceptions among the Billionaire and especially tech Billionaire set). We don't produce a lot of people with lifestyles like those under Medici patronage because so few of us have the monetary cushion to support "idle speculation" and time intensive work. We aren't even living paycheck to paycheck, we are often living three or four paychecks behind, which binds us to our jobs and to normal, systematized work in a way more reminiscent of the Company Towns of the early 20th century than the free and mobile society that we purport to live in.

In this context the complaint that lack of money, specifically the lack of deep monetary cushions produced by high rates of savings, coherent investing and reduced consumption of commodity goods becomes quite obvious. This class of entrepreneurials, like many of us, is caught up in a culture that no longer holds thrift and accumulation as a virtue and as a result often has no idea what a life looks like without a brand new car every three years or the newest cell phone every 12 months. Insofar as this prevents them from having the time, space, and ability to create, this aspect of the modern system of innovation is criminal.

Speaking of time...

40 Hours a Week

After sleep, which takes up about 9 hours of our day according to the Bureau of Labor Statistics, work is our next biggest time sync. On average we work 5.74 hours a day or 40.18 hours a week, a massive portion of our lives and productive energy.

This 40 hour work schedule has existed unchanged since the late 1800s when labor activists and Unions fought to establish an eight hour work day. Before that, it was not unheard of for factory workers to be forced to work ten or more hours, six days a week under often dangerous conditions. After years of strikes, including the Illinois strike of 1867 which managed to shut down an entire city, and the Chicago riots of 1886 in which prominent labor activists were rounded up, jailed and executed after a bomb went off in Haymarket Square, the first Federal Law establishing an eight hour work day for large groups of workers was passed in 1916 with the establishment of the Adamson Act, which regulated work times for railroad workers and provided overtime pay for anyone working over eight hours a day. These laws came to a head with the Fair Labor Standards Act of 1937 under the New Deal, which provided an eight hour work day to employees covering about 20% of the U.S. labor force. This was a major win for workers of the time. Since much of the work available was in mining, manufacturing and constructions projects like railroads -- reducing the work day to a manageable length saved lives. It reduced workplace accidents, it reduced the terrible stresses on the workers bodies and it reduced the ability of managers to treat workers more as indentured serfs than paid employees.

Subsequent research has shown that reducing the number of hours worked might have also increased the efficiency of the work itself. As early as 1908, pioneering researchers like Ernst Abbe had discovered that reducing work hours from nine to eight actually increased industrial output. Henry Ford was famous for taking this kind of research to heart, in 1926, well before the Fair Labor Standards Act, he enacted a policy of reduced hours in his factories. He cut his employee's work day from ten to eight hours and their work week from six to five days, after twelve years of experiments he found that by doing so he actually increased worker output and reduced production costs. The idea that he stumbled upon was that not every hour of production is the same, human beings get tired and as we get tired we become less productive, we make more mistakes and we start burning time rather than using it. Anyone who has ever found themselves at the end of a long work day simply staring blankly at their computer screen can easily relate.

The eight hour work day was a grand victory for organized labor, but in the nearly 80 years since it was enacted, we seemed to have forgotten its basic lessons. In the world of software development, especially game design, many companies now ask their employees to devote 60, 70, and sometimes even 80 hours a week towards projects during crunch periods. In high powered law firms, investment banks and other professional organizations it's not unheard of for employees to work 65 hour weeks in the office, and many more hours outside of it. This slow creeping up of work hours has even started to affect normal, white collar employment in offices and corporations. With the labor market tight, employers cutting costs, and the addition of technologies like smartphones which allow employees to never really leave the office, more time and more commitment is expected of workers today than since the heyday of modern labor abuse in the 19th century.

What has this cost us?

First and foremost it can be argued that much of this additional work time is not particularly productive. Significantly increased work hours lead to increases in error rates for workers. In fact, simple sleep deprivation can have massive effects. In 1997, for example, Colonel Gregory Belenky of the Division of Neuropsychiatry at Walter Reed Army Institute of Research showed that for every 24 hours of continuous wakefulness cognitive function decreased by 25%. In his sleep deprivation studies he found that soldiers under the effects of sleep deprivation would fire on friendly targets if asked to, rather than reviewing the situation map and speaking out against the bad orders. These same soldiers, during a 4 hour sleep schedule, would fire less than a third of the rounds of soldiers under a 7 hour sleep schedule. If employees are working twice as much then, a lot of those extra hours are being drawn from time they might otherwise be sleeping, under these conditions it's unlikely that they will be producing their best work.

The second cost is one more relevant to our discussion, and that is what happens when these workers go home. Not every hour is created equal and by expending their most productive hours and even most of their moderately productive hours at work, they have little additional energy to learn, analyze or create. This goes a long way towards explaining the next biggest time sync, leisure (4 hours a day), usually in the form of television or other screen activities. When we add those hours to the pool we are essentially "out of time" to do anything more productive than errands or other lifestyle maintenance tasks. This is a poisonous environment for our class of entrepreneurials because if we know nothing else about those who we would call polymaths, it is that they had time. Time not only to develop their skills, but time to analyze and think deeply about their subjects of interest.

Albert Einstein famously developed the Theory of Relativity through years of subtle, continuous imaginings. Einstein was not a bench scientist for most of his life, instead he relied on the analogies and mental models that he had developed. To understand one aspect of Relativity he imagined riding on a light beam, to understand another he imagined chasing his brother through space, signaling him with a flash light and how this would be perceived from different reference frames. These kinds of models can only be created and refined when one has time and energy to do so. Nassim Taleb explains in his book *Antifragile* that this time for reflection was the result of what he calls the Bar Bell model, in which one covers his basic needs using a risk-less endeavor so that he can devote time to an extremely risky, high reward one. Einstein choose to work at a patents office, a notoriously slow paced career that allowed him a great deal of time to think and imagine, it also gave him access to new ideas as they passed over his desk. In addition, because he had a stable job that took up little of his productive energy, he was essentially under the patronage of the government. His basic lifestyle was paid for by his salary, his energy was his own to use, and thus he was able to devote a monumental amount of time to his work in theoretical physics.

For many of us this strategy is not available. Our jobs expect more of us and do not provide compensation large enough to cover our desire for consumption. Our culture of consumption drives us towards devoting even more time to work in an effort to have more money to spend on more commodity goods. Since we only have so many productive hours in the day, by the time we are done with this treadmill what we are left with are minds that can do little more than passively absorb whatever information is easiest to consume, usually in the form of the latest reality television show or YouTube phenomenon. For the class caught up in this system, even if they have the desire to do more, many of them simply do not have energy to make it happen and they certainly do not have the huge amount of time to develop the skills they need to give them a real shot at being successful.

Skills, Mastery and the Liberal Arts

In classical antiquity the "liberal arts" included those skills that were considered essential for a free person to participate in civic life. For the ancient Greeks they were grammar, rhetoric and logic. The Medieval Church expanded them to include arithmetic, geometry, music and astronomy, which they referred to as the Quadrivium (with the initial Greek conception being referred to as the Trivium). By the 5th Century, writers like Martianus Capella were defining the seven Liberal Arts as: grammar, rhetoric, music, astronomy, geometry, dialectic and arithmetic. The core idea of these Arts was to create a class of people who were broadly informed and capable of participating in every level of civic discourse. Unlike the "slave classes," these men would be articulate, knowledgeable and virtuous. Universities that implemented this model relied heavily on the teachings of philosophers like Socrates and Aristotle, and focused much of their attention not on developing employees with specific skills useful for a narrow set of tasks, but citizens capable of learning and adapting to whichever tasks were set before them.

A part of this conceit was the result of the types of people who attended Universities up through the middle part of the 20th Century. The only people who could afford the time and money necessary for such a high level of education were the scions of the wealthy. These men were being groomed not as merchants and craftsmen, but as leaders and were being given the skills they'd need to take their place in society. It is little wonder then that many famous polymaths like Issac Newton and Charles Darwin were trained, for at least some portion of their lives, under this regime.

In the realm of scientific inquiry, before the 19th Century, the idea of the scientist as we would conceive of it today was unheard of. Instead, those who inquired into the nature of things referred to themselves as natural philosophers. According to Mortimer Adler in *The Four Dimensions of Philosophy: Metaphysical, Moral, Objective, Categorical*, a Natural Philosopher was one who studied astronomy, cosmology, nature on a grand scale; causes, the elements, infinity, matter, mechanics, natural qualities, physical quantities, the relationship of physical entities, chance, probability and the philosophy of space and time among other pursuits. Many of those following this discipline would have also found themselves in a University system that relied heavily on the classical liberal arts. The result would be something antithetical to our modern society, the almost fully unfocused man.

The knowledge that they acquired, above all else, was a framework that held that acquiring knowledge was a virtue. They learned how to learn and were placed into a structure that promoted broad, varied and life long study not merely as something that was desirable but as an ethical standard for a fully realized life. They were taught to seek answers and ask questions, and were given the mandate to go out into the world and find those answers wherever they might turn out to be. Their relative wealth and privilege, like a Medici patronage, secured for them the time to follow these pursuits. The result was that many, such as Newton, found themselves moving fluidly between such disparate fields as optics and alchemy, and all of the polymaths chased passions ranging from writing to politics to mathematics, sometimes in the same breath. While this mode of unfocused inquiry is not nearly as efficient as specialization, especially when we are speaking about the sorts of specialized knowledge required to participate in the massively expensive projects generated by Big Science and corporate research, this class of seekers is incredibly valuable for setting a direction for that research to follow, and for generating the kinds of innovative questions that one only can when he has a wide base of knowledge to draw from.

But what about the technical skills?

10,000 Hours

Malcolm Gladwell asserts in his book *Outliers* that it takes about 10,000 hours of practice to become an expert at a skill. He makes his case by pointing to examples such as the time the Beatles spent between 1960 and 1964 playing concerts in dive bars in Hamburg, Germany, and Bill Gates who, through the luck of his circumstances, was able to start tinkering with computer programming in 1968, years before most of his peers would even see a computer in action let alone play around with one. These experts were able to clock their "10,000 hours" early in life and thus had a major head start when they later brought their skills to bear as professionals. This "10,000" rule is based on research by Anders Ericsson of Florida State University, who studied concert violinists at the Berlin Academy of Music. What he found was that the highest performers were those who were able to surpass the 10,000 hour mark early in their careers and that performance decreased linearly as the number of hours fell.

As Ericsson explains it though, this 10,000 hour marker is not a magic number and not just any hours count. In order for it to be productive, the person has to be practicing deliberately with the goal of improving his skills. Playing the theme from Star Wars ten thousand times on the piano, for example, does not a virtuoso make. In order to grow in skills you have to work for a very, very long time at just that and continually challenge yourself.

The interesting thing is that for all their lack of focus, the polymath is much more likely to be able to achieve this more subtle goal than the modern specialist. The specialist is taught to do a single set of things very, very well and spends most of his career doing just that -- over and over again in only slightly different ways. As a result, he never achieves real mastery, except in the very narrow field that his years of practice has made rote. The polymath, the natural philosopher, the person who existed and thrived under the system of classical liberal arts training and its precursors was trained to seek out and overcome challenges, to approach the acquisition of knowledge and skills deliberately and to look for new answers and new questions. Like the Beatles, they were practitioners, producing products and ideas, getting feedback from their peers and seeking out ways to overcome the issues raised by their detractors, and fortunately for them, this is just the kind of deliberate, active practice that leads to mastery.

Without an intellectual edifice that encourages knowledge and learning above rote skill acquisition, many of our lost entrepreneurials feel trapped by whatever box that their Major and their career path has placed them inside. They feel that if they are biologists, learning about programming is a waste of time. They feel that if they are managers, data analysis skills are meaningless. They can no longer separate themselves from the artificially constructed roles that society has developed for them, and as a result even if they can see the skills that they would need to make their products a reality, they do not have the confidence to pursue them, because they are deeply afraid that by doing so they will open themselves up to the derision of their peers (for wasting time) and lose the utter, mechanical focus they believe they need to advance in their chosen field. When combined with a lack of energy and a lack of financial cushion, all the incentives begin to point away from innovation and towards a system that promotes, above all else, stasis.

A Cry for Help

Now perhaps, our three excuses begin to seem more reasonable, a cry for help rather than a white flag.

It's not that these innovators need "money," not in the concrete sense that they need money to buy a sandwich or pay their rent, what they need is financial cushion, that far more ineffable quality in which money ceases to be the primary focus of their endeavors. They don't need to be rich (by modern standards) in order to achieve this, they just need to have enough, enough money to support their lifestyle and a little more besides to insulate themselves against shocks and provide them with time. They also need to craft a lifestyle that values creation over consumption, reducing the need to have a cushion so large that it's practically impossible to achieve.

It's not that these potential entrepreneurs need more "time". What they need is a system that taxes their creative energy less completely. They are working and working up to the red line, burning away their creative capacity to nothing, and by the time they get home they are left stripped of the kinds of energy they need to think deeply about anything beyond how much sleep they need, and how quickly they can usher the kids into bed. These people need their own Bar Bell models, new methods of working that allow them to pay their bills on one hand and work on their high risk, high reward projects on the other. This means changing the way they think about work, not as a treadmill towards ever more focused versions of the same activities, but as a means to an end. A way of gathering resources to be used for bigger and better things.

These dreamers do need more "skills" but the skills they need are the core values of the classical liberal education, the ethic that learning is a virtue and that in order to be a fully realized person they must challenge themselves constantly. It's the skills epitomized by the Beatles and Gates, people who established a goal for themselves and sought out new ways to outdo themselves. They did not simply play the same twelve notes over and over again until they perfected them, they had feedback and consequences and every time they created they learned about their defects and worked to rise above them. By learning how to learn, and having a structure that rewarded that learning, gathering the technical skills that they needed was just a matter of focused practice, and having the confidence to work outside of the narrow boxes that society had built for them.

As thinkers, as builders, as doers, as a society that lionizes creation and innovation and needs our creators to be risk takers and change makers, we need to find a way to make this happen, to create a world where this lost class is not left to wallow in their reality television and dead-end jobs, to make it practical for those with drive and ability to express their talents, to raise the already slim odds that we can create new entries in the history books. We need to recreate the template of the polymath for the modern world, not to replace the system of specialization but to support and improve upon it, to provide it with guidance and models of excellence, to give radical innovation a chance to thrive. We know this. We all do. Now the question is what are we going to do about it?

Part 3

Rebuilding the Polymath

To begin discussing how we might solve this problem we must first establish what we are not trying to do.

We are not trying to recreate systems of patronage, which when all is said and done were the result of the radical concentration of wealth and influence in the hands of a trivially small population of elites, who simply found it in their best interests to spread that wealth in a way that would maximize their social cache.

We are not trying to recreate the University system of the ancient world to the mid 20th century, which was, at the best of times, exclusionary and insular, limiting access to education to those who the system deemed to be "worthy" of being proper citizens.

We are not trying to replace Big Science with it's smaller more shiftless cousin or modern, systematized work with some kind of Athenian society of "thinkers." These older models were overturned for a reason, and their larger more regimented replacements have done good on a massive scale, allowing more people to be gainfully employed rather than marginalized, and larger and more complex scientific endeavors to be undertaken.

No, we are not interested in any of these things, instead what we want is to take a close look at these historical models and extract some part of what made them effective, and use that to create a new system with modern values that will allow more people to do more innovative work.

To this end, we return to our three "excuses":

If only I had more money...
If only I had more time...
If only I had more skills...

And begin to look at what can be done to improve things.

Means to an End?

Why do we work? Why do we save? Ask these questions and the most common answer you'll receive is that we work to pay bills and we save for emergencies and retirement. This seems reasonable enough until you begin to look at the essential trade offs of this paradigm. As we discussed, work in the modern sense provides powerful disincentives for innovators, draining both productive time along with physical and psychological energy. 40, 60, 80 hours a week of basically rote tasks also grossly inhibits opportunities for skill development, further reducing the chance that even if they do find the time to explore a topic and build out a project from it, that it will be successful.

This idea of working and saving towards a period in which you retire from the job market is a fairly modern one. Retirement as a concept is an extraordinarily recent invention, the first system of retirement only being introduced in Germany in the 1880s. Before that, people were forced to work up until they died due to a combination of low life expectancy and no formalized system of pensions to fund their period of idleness. While the idea of working until you simply could not anymore led to broad abuses, it also provided an incentive, especially for the already wealthy (not necessarily by modern standards), to find ways to limit the system's ability to affect them.

The "gentlemen scientist" is one plausible result of this, men like Henry Fox Talbot and James Lovelock, many of which participated in scientific organizations like the Royal Society, used their wealth, either inherited or gathered during an earlier part of their formal career, to buy themselves time and freedom for independent scientific inquiry.

Henry Talbot (1800 - 1877) is a classic example, an inventor by trade he spent his early life working as a commercial photographer in Britain. He parlayed this into a scientific career which included significant communication with the Royal Society on topics related to mathematics. This led, after a series of scientific experiments, to his development of the calotype process, a precursor to more modern photographic processes. Talbot's life and work represent an application of a bar bell model, he used commercial photography to fund research, research that once completed lead to a product that allowed him to devote his time to further scientific inquiry.

Lovelock provides us with a more modern example, much like Talbot he had early work in a photography firm. Lovelock's next stop, however, was an engagement with NASA where he worked to develop scientific instruments. Later still, in 1974, he was elected a fellow at the Royal Society. During this entire period he used the freedom these engagements afforded him to develop innovations like the Gaia Hypothesis, which proposes that that the biosphere is a self regulating entity. Like Einstein in the patent office, Lovelock choose a profession that enhanced rather than distracted from his real passions, and that also left him with sufficient amounts of energy and financial stability to devote his free time to create.

These models provide us with two new goals for the working polymath. Instead of working simply to maintain his lifestyle, he works so that he can enhance his skills and have time to develop riskier projects, and instead of saving (a tiny amount in the U.S.) so that he can retire in 40 years, he saves aggressively now so that he can afford to work less later and devote his energy to his passions.

The Ethic of Thrift

How much savings is enough? In 2011 Russell Research came up with a rule of thumb that provides us with a good place to start, they call it TRI 30. Given an approximately 30 year savings horizon, you can be 90% certain to achieve a replacement rate of X% of your current income by saving at a rate of X*30%. For example, if you currently make $100,000 a year and you want to make $60,000 a year (a 60% replacement rate) during retirement, you need to save 60%*30% or 18% of your income. This is a far cry from the 4% rate that has become the norm, and yet still does not achieve the goal we posed earlier. We are not saving to retire to Florida at 65, we are saving to have the financial cushion to create as soon as possible.

To achieve this, we need to find a way to be more aggressive still, and in order to make that realistic we need to start looking at crafting a lifestyle based less on heavy consumption and more on thrift.

Thrift does not necessarily mean asceticism. The ascetics, from early Christian groups to Buddhists and Jainists use thrift along with various other self denials as a means in and of itself, a way to purify themselves spiritually or as a sacrifice to their god or spiritual calling. Thrift for our purposes is simply a process of recognizing how money flows in and out of our lives, and through that process developing the discipline to make choices that free us from the cycles of debt and consumption that limit our ability to save.

Let's look at a more concrete example. According to the Bureau of Labor Statistics, the average household where both individuals earned Bachelor's degrees made approximately $73,446 and spent $48,109 excluding taxes and debt service. The Tax Foundation estimates that after deductions and credits a family making this amount would spend an additional 7% ($5,141) on taxes so that when all is said and done they would be left with about $20,000. This represents a potential savings rate of 27%. If every dime of this was invested every year at 6% for 15 years this family would have $420,000 in the bank. While this is not an immense amount of wealth by modern standards, what it can provide is peace of mind, which often is enough, enough to allow this household to take risks that one steeped in debt or living paycheck to paycheck simply could not.

Averages are tricky things though, and the issue faced by many households is that that their expenses (including debt service) are well beyond this BLS number. Where does all that money go? Usually to one of four places: housing, food, transportation or insurance. These four expenses make up the vast majority of what people spend and given the sheer size and persistence of these expenses are likely the only practical levers we have to affect our rates of savings. Excluding food and insurance, which are necessities we would prefer not to fiddle with, practically speaking what's left is that many of us are living in houses we can't afford with property taxes that are too high, and driving around in cars that are beyond our means to pay for.

It's not hard to see how this happens, if you increase your mortgage payment from $1,200 a month to $1,700 and add a $400 a month car payment, suddenly the $20,000 you would have had left over at the end of the year is cut in half. Add to that the additional money required for taxes, maintenance and the associated lifestyle changes of living in a much nicer place and the end result is limited to no room to save.

For the modern model that values current consumption over future creative capacity this is simply the cost of doing business, for those of us who wish to have the ability to take risks and innovate, this is a trap that we need to understand and take steps to undermine. We need to choose homes that we can afford in areas that are affordable. Instead of buying the biggest house our credit rating will allow, we should start by asking ourselves how much room we really need and why. Once we have a clear idea of the scale and type of home that we need, we should try to find the most affordable option that fits that criteria even if that means living in a place that is smaller or an area that is less opulent than we might otherwise be able to afford. In terms of transportation, we must remember that cars are probably the worst financial investment that a person can make, losing much of their value the moment they are driven off the lot. Ultimately, we need to do better at balancing our desire for status against our goals of being free of debt and financially secure.

That being said, while we are strongly against taking on most kinds of debt, there is one category whose rewards, given the correct mindset, might far outstrip its potential risks.

The Last Patron

Much has been said about student loans, much that we would agree with, often students take on mind boggling amounts of debt to fund their education, and in an economic environment that rewards fewer and fewer degree programs (primarily STEM and the professional degrees) this debt is often difficult or impossible to repay. Student loans are, however, responsible for something of immense value beyond the education that students receive, student loans provide us with what might be the last remaining system of patronage.

Between scholarships and loans, a large number of students in the U.S. have completely or near completely deferred the costs of their housing and education for upwards of four years. For those students who go into PHD programs, this period can be much longer. Entrepreneurs from Bill Gates to Larry Page to Mark Zuckerberg realized the value of this deferment. Like the artists that built masterpieces under the Medici, this period of relative financial security provided them with time and space to think and create. More than that, it put them in a context to find like-minded collaborators. If Larry Page had not met Sergei Brin at Stanford, it is unlikely that Google would exist. If Mark Zuckerberg had not been exposed to the social dynamics of Harvard, Facebook may never have been built. Silicon Valley itself was the result of recognizing the power of smart, driven students to use their ample free time to research and produce commercial products.

If students loans are taken as an investment then, a means of trading future debt for current time, they can be an extremely powerful way to kick start innovation. Especially if the education that you purchase using those loans serves to enhance and inform your future projects.

The modern polymath then is left with two paths towards having the financial wherewithal to create. The first begins the moment she enters the University system, where she must realize the power and patronage that this system has provided her with and take advantage of it to develop a solid foundation on which she can build out future projects. This means doing research, finding collaborators and tinkering with prototypes all in an effort to refine the skills and make the mistakes that will lead to greater, future success. The second begins right after graduation, where she needs to make choices about where she lives, what she drives, and how much money she will spend to maintain her lifestyle -- choices that should lean heavily towards thrift and savings, not for some period of retirement 40 years off but instead so that like the "gentlemen scientists" of the Royal Society she will have a nest egg large enough for her to take risks. She needs to cultivate a new virtue, the virtue of less, and develop a clear understanding of what's truly important to her.

Now that we have a better understanding of the money, we need to start finding the time. To do that, we'll need to take a trip.

Bar Bell Models

Take a flight to Los Angeles and wander into any restaurant on or near Hollywood Blvd. Take a seat. Browse the menu for a moment and look around you. If it's a decent place, by the time you finish taking in the crowd of screen writers and models-to-be your waiter will have arrived. Before you give him your order, ask him his name. Small talk will likely ensue, which should give you the perfect opening to ask the question that brought you to this restaurant in the first place. Ask him why he's here. Seven out of ten says that he will tell you he's doing the "acting thing" and that he's working in this restaurant to make ends meat in the meantime. Give him your order, enjoy your food and leave a big tip.

What you've just witnessed is a partial answer to the problem of Time. Acting, especially in Hollywood, is an endless series of auditions and agent meetings, networking and disappointments. To try to make it big and hold down a full time job would be nearly impossible, so those who are making a go at it often fund their dreams through a series of part time jobs working in restaurants, coffee shops and other places with flexible schedules. For these creative professions, the idea of working as a means to an ends rather than as an ends in and of itself is alive and well. While most of these men and women will end up disappointed, for the ones who make it, there is almost no better way.

The suggestion here is not to quit whatever it is that you are doing and start working at Starbucks while you tinker around with your start up. Remember, in order to make any of this work you need to have the financial cushion that only some kind of sustained employment can provide you with. What we are suggesting is that you begin to integrate the lessons of the Bar Bell model into your career goals. Namely, you should find a job that either enhances your future goals as an innovator, as was the case with Henry Talbot's photography career, or one that leaves you with enough time and energy to devote to your craft, as was the case with Einstein and is the case with many of the actors and actresses in Hollywood.

More tactically, the aspiring polymath should avoid any job that consumes more than 40 hours a week of his time unless that job provides him with useful, actionable skills like the endless hours the Beatles played in Germany did. As mentioned earlier, 40 hours is about the limit of our productive capacity and if your job is taking up more than that, you are severely limiting your ability to create. The aspiring polymath should also, where possible, avoid permanent employment entirely, instead parlaying his skills as a consultant or freelancer. These types of careers can provide you with significantly more time and if setup correctly will allow you to make a schedule that gives you the ability to both work and create.

Paul Graham, co-founder of Viaweb and later yCombinator took this latter lesson to heart. Early in his career, Paul realized that while he was a skilled software developer, his real passion was painting. After earning his PHD in applied science at Harvard, he went on to study the subject at the Rhode Island School of Design and the Academia di Belle Arti in Florence. He then spent much of his early career taking on a variety of IT consulting engagements, earning enough money to live on, and then painting until the cash ran out. According to Robert Greene in his book *Mastery* -- Viaweb, which was sold to Yahoo! for $46 million worth of stock, was partially an attempt to get off of this treadmill -- he grew to dislike consulting and wanted to find a way to earn enough money so that he could devote time to his passions. Paul understood that work needed to lead somewhere, and that time was critically important to determining where that somewhere was. He used his talents not to solidify his position on the treadmill but to ultimately overcome it, and he used freelance work to buy him time to make that happen.

The answer for the burgeoning polymath then is a form of progressive entrepreneurship. This might begin as a full time career, a job that earns you enough money to develop your skills and save. You work in this job for just long enough to build up a nest egg, at which point you can move on to devoting your full efforts to innovation. Depending on your skill set, this period could also take the form of a Bar Bell model, where you either take on part time employment or freelance engagements in order to better shape your schedule and allow you more time to devote to creative work. In either case, you use your free hours to innovate and create with the goal of building something that will allow you the option of getting off the treadmill entirely and giving all your time over to entrepreneurial pursuits.

Finally we return to the problem of skills and how our modern polymath might approach mastering them.

Breaking the Box

In 1714 the British Parliament had a problem, namely, they needed an accurate way to measure longitude. Proper measures of longitude, along with latitude, would allow ships to correctly orient themselves at sea, a critical ability during transatlantic voyages where inaccurate measurements could lead to dangerous errors of navigation. Latitude was significantly easier, as all you really needed was the altitude of the sun at noon, then you could apply a table which would give you the sun's declination for the day. Longitude, however, became exceedingly difficult to measure once you sailed beyond the sight of land, as previous methods of dead reckoning failed to produce accurate results at those distances.

Without a clear solution in sight, Parliament established the Longitude Act in 1714 and through this created the Board of Longitude whose purpose was to administer an incentive prize which would award up to 20,000 pounds to anyone who could contribute significantly to the development of a method to make this measurement accurately.

Many of the best minds of the time, including such stalwarts as Issac Newton, failed to come up with a solution. In the end, the answer was arrived at by John Harrison, a self taught watchmaker who created the first marine chronometer.

This was not the first or the last time a relative unknown with an odd skill set would spearhead a major innovation. The Wright Brothers, remembered as the creators of the first airplane capable of sustained, powered flight were complete unknowns in the burgeoning field of aviation. By trade, they were bicycle makers, and they used the skills that they developed to come to a radical conclusion. Up until this point, airplane designers were focused on making their vehicles as stable as possible. This meant that the person flying these early planes had little control over the vehicle in flight, leading to a number of spectacular accidents. What the Wright Brothers understood that these men didn't was that bicycles, another human powered, inherently unstable system could be brought under control by human operators as long as they were given the freedom to re-balance themselves. The result of this innovation was the first plane to successfully fly on December 13th 1903.

There are two lessons we can draw from these examples, the first is that often it's broad-based competition that is the mother of great innovation, and the second is that great innovators are often those who can combine skills from disparate fields into entirely novel solutions. This latter lesson is also the lesson of the Classical Liberal Arts, where students were taught the ethic of learning, made to study such far flung subjects as music, geometry and astronomy and then challenged by convention and social mores to apply these skills towards great deeds.

This brings us to how a polymath might approach knowledge. While academia does continue to provide students with opportunities to learn a wide variety of subjects, the ethic of knowledge acquisition as a means toward developing wisdom rather than a means of developing technical skills is lacking. Students are encouraged to define themselves by their major, which severely limits their ability to think beyond that major and pick up additional skills which might prove invaluable to uncovering true innovations. Henry Talbot was a photographer with a distinct interest in mathematics and invention, he along with many other polymaths were successful in some part because the barriers between scientific pursuits were far more fluid, which gave them the freedom to learn broadly and apply deeply. John Harrison and the Wright Brothers, because they were mostly self-taught and thus lacked the formal constraints of academia, were able to see outside of their expertise and apply their skills to novel problems.

The polymath then should be a broad consumer of knowledge,

not confined to any particular academic box. While she should have a specialty (if only for practical purposes) she should read and consume media far afield of that specialty. This could take the form of reading books about linguistics and neuroscience to bolster her knowledge of Marketing, or watching documentaries on education and economics to help give context to the products she develops as an Engineer. Perhaps she can do what Paul Graham did and cultivate a passion for an art like painting, while pursuing a career as a software developer. The point is to acquire broad knowledge, find connections and exploit those connections to create innovations.

Knowledge to her should be fuel for creation, and technical skills should be pursued that will allow her to disseminate that information effectively. In today's world -- programming, statistics, communication, and web based skills are foundational (along with many others). The point is not for her to be an expert in any of these skills, but to be competent in all of them along with whatever specialty she has devoted her academic time to. This is another major change in the way we currently think about skill acquisition. As it stands, we want to learn more and more about less and less, which is fantastic for those who want to further a career in a very narrow profession, however, for the inventors and innovators out there a different approach is often necessary -- they need to value competence over expertise and try to achieve competence in as many technical skills as they will need to achieve their goals, even if those skills are as far ranging as Newton's love of both astronomy and alchemy.

The big caveat here returns us to what Anders Ericsson explained earlier when describing how one develops mastery over a skill, the point is not simply to do a thing but to do a thing deliberately, with the purpose of developing competence. To do this one needs both focus and feedback.

Thesis, Feedback, Revision

The polymath's of old achieved feedback by near constant letter writing. The Royal Society and similar organizations around this time used letters as a means for scientists, who often spent their time afield, to communicate their ideas to their peers and receive critiques. This is similar to our current model of academic peer review, but whereas that has become a rather mechanical process designed to codify academic advancement, the letters of the Royal Society were intimate exchanges between friends and rivals which helped both sets of people to refine their ideas down to fine points.

For the modern polymath the solution is to be constantly sharing ideas and seeking out feedback. This is not necessarily the rapid spit-balling of twitter posts, but instead the premise of being more transparent with the results of tinkering. Tinkering allows you to take knowledge and transform it into something concrete, and broad transparency forces you to get feedback on those ideas, feedback that can be used to improve them. Polymaths should be builders and sharers, people with the self confidence to develop an idea, make a mistake in public, and keep working to make that idea better.

As for focus, the incentive prize gives us an especially useful model. The Ansari X Prize, developed by serial entrepreneur Peter Diamandis, is responsible for creating the first commercial space vehicle, and today the X Prize Foundation is working on dozens of other competitions in fields ranging from environmental protection to medicine. Why are these prizes so useful? By providing a concrete problem and a structured goal they help to focus the efforts of a wide range of innovators, people who might never have participated in a particular research field are often willing to look at the problem when presented as a challenge. The British Parliament learned this lesson well when a watchmaker solved their Longitude problem. Of course, you don't need to go out and vie for the X Prize in order to challenge and focus yourself, but you do need concrete goals to test yourself against. As a polymath, you should be constantly striving towards improving your skills through practical application and ensuring those applications are deliberately focused on increasing competence and mastery.

The answer to the skill question then comes down to focused goal setting, constant feedback, and progressive challenges. For the polymath, skills are not simple technical abilities specialized for the completion of a narrow band of tasks, skills should be developed deliberately and broadly to provide the polymath with the breadth of knowledge and range of talents necessary to make innovative connections. To this end, the polymath is the consummate tinkerer, acquiring knowledge, developing a thesis, testing that thesis and sharing the results with her peers to get feedback and refine her knowledge for the next round of tinkering.

So is that it then? We have the money, we have the time, and we have the skills. Have we completely defined the modern polymath? Let's see...

The Polymath Defined

Broadly we can characterize a modern polymath as a person who...

Strives to be an innovator, drawing on disparate knowledge, making novel connections and pushing the boundaries of the possible.

Uses thrift as a means to design a lifestyle free from the treadmill of purchases, debt and the overwork needed to fuel it.

Saves aggressively and invests rationally in order to create the financial cushion necessary to take risks.

Understands that all work and all employment is a means rather than an ends, and seeks out types of work that enhance her ability to create.

Believes in the ethic of learning, making a virtue of broad understanding over narrow specialization with the goal of directing that understanding towards great works.

Challenges her skills, achieving mastery through constant application, feedback and revision.

More than all of that though, she is a template for other innovators to emulate, a person who understands that the boxes we've built for ourselves should be signposts rather than constraints and one who is willing to ignore them completely or even subvert them if necessary to create radical change. She uses Big Science and Big Industry for what they are good for, industrial scale production of technological and commercial change, while using small science and tinkering to guide that change towards more useful goals. She creates out loud, challenging conventions and sharing mistakes, always looking for new ways of applying old knowledge. Above all else she is a doer, who believes that knowledge without application is hollow and that the goal of a well lived life is to apply her knowledge towards big problems.

She is something that our world today needs a lot more of.

Part 4
Conclusions and Introductions

We've traveled a long way in the last few sections, from the Greek Trivium to the Ansari X Prize and I think now it's time for you to learn something about Innovate GSB, who we are, and how we are working to rebuild the polymath.

First, allow me to lay out our thesis --

We are working to recreate the spirit of multidisciplinary exploration and tinkering in innovation. To provide a space for the brilliant generalist, the broad minded inventor, the thinkers and doers that don't quite fit into our increasingly hyper-specialized economic environment to thrive. We want to build tools that improve lives, and build tool makers able to wield complexity in all its forms and apply it big problems.

Ultimately, we want to spearhead projects and build out ideas that will free innovators to create, and provide them with the tools, skills and inspiration they need to create well. By doing this we want to create a world that integrates the speed and scale epitomized by Big Science with the radical, free-form and powerful innovations driven by broad minded polymaths.

How are we going to do this?

ProjectMONA. This project, spearheaded by Steve Spalding is looking to tackle both the skill and money problem from the perspective of those just entering the workforce. The idea here is two fold, first he wants to build up a knowledge base around questions of saving, investing, health, programming and web development along with a broad range of recommended reading and media. The idea here is to introduce potential polymaths to the skill sets they'll need to go from thinkers and dreamers to tinkerers and doers, and to provide them with the broad competencies they'll need to do everything from developing a financial cushion to stepping outside of the stringent academic boxes they might still find themselves in.

The second goal of the project is to bring these people together in a network, a network designed for the purpose of discussing ideas, developing thesis' and producing products. The important point here is that the network is not simply about discussion it's about doing, it's about using the skills developed from the knowledge base and applying them to real problems, problems geared towards improving lives.

Klever. Miguel Barbosa is approaching the time and skill problem with his project Klever. Klever is also broken into two parts, with the first part being an interview series that Miguel is currently producing with well known authors, scientists and academics. The point here is to recreate a small piece of the system of Classical Liberal Arts, providing a range of people with access to the ideas of great contemporary thinkers. He wants to take this one step further, and work to codify and catalog some of the ideas that these thinkers are interested in seeing developed, ideas they perhaps don't have time to transform into products on their own.

He then wants to bring these thinkers together in a network where they can meet and share. Like the Royal Society and other scientific organizations of earlier times, the idea here is to take people with disparate knowledge and give them a venue to share their that knowledge with their peers.

The ultimate goal of this pair of projects is to introduce these Klever thinkers to the burgeoning polymaths being produced in ProjectMONA. By allowing these broad-minded tinkerers to have access to the specialized knowledge and thoughts of great scientists and academics, they feel that they can open up entirely new avenues for innovation.

CoralEight. CoralEight is being lead by James Gibson and it's designed as an information marketplace. The idea here is that a large part of the problem with data acquisition is finding reasonable ways to match those who have the data with those who are in need of it. CoralEight seeks to make this process more transparent, and by doing so provide researchers, academics, corporations and individuals with cheaper, faster access to data sets.

From the standpoint of the collectors, he wants to turn data acquisition into a more active process. Like the naturalists and biologists of the 19th century did with their letters and field books, he wants to give people more incentive to collect and share data-sets of all kinds, and provide them with a storehouse and marketplace to get feedback on the data that they are collecting. The project also seeks to get insights on how all of this data is valued, from personal details to the weather in Boise, Idaho. By doing so he hopes to encourage the free spread of data and to incentivize those doing the spreading.

The iGSB Toolkit. This is an ongoing project lead up by all members of the partnership that seeks to create a set of useful tools that will provide people with better ways to approach saving, investing, health, wellness, and entrepreneurship. In general they want to make tools that help people to understand choices and their consequences, all backed by insights from science. They feel that time, money and skill problems are often problems of information, and that by providing simple tools that give people better access to this kind of information they can move towards helping them escape these traps.

Letters. What you are reading right now is a template for the sorts of letters that iGSB wishes to create. Most will be much shorter than this, but all will attempt to provide members, stakeholders and the general public with different ways of thinking about innovation and insights into why iGSB approaches problems as it does. We hope that these letters will provide value far beyond simply updating you on the comings and goings of the partnership, we hope that they will give you reason to pause and reason to think, and most importantly provide you with a reason to begin corresponding with us. We understand and treasure the value of feedback, and more than anything we want to provide a venue to propose radical new ways of thinking and have them critiqued and explored.

So after reading this we would love to hear your thoughts, you can reach me, Steve Spalding, at steve@innovategsb.com.

Appendix

Ultimately any manifesto is incomplete without a next step. For us, that step is in fact two steps, and this appendix has been designed to provide you with the guidance necessary to achieve both. The first of these is grounded in the ideas of the Classical Liberal Arts, namely, that innovation, the kinds of innovation we are trying to induce, is born from those with broad competencies across a variety of subjects. Unlike the Greeks and the Medievals that came after them, we are somewhat less interested in diving into the rich abstractions of philosophy or the stark beauty of geometry and mathematics as our modern educational system has made it its mission to drive those lessons home. Instead, since our mission is to create innovations that help improve the lives of people, we want to look at burgeoning fields that help us to better understand how people function within a technological society.

To that end, many of the resources we provide in this appendix will deal with research and insights from the social sciences, behavioral economics, irrationality, evolution, neuroscience, the history and future of technology, money, finance, along with explorations of predictions, forecasting and risk. We want to provide you with deeper insights into how information, broadly defined to include everything from risk to bytes to biases, flows and is interpreted within human systems, along with a grounding in the historical and social context in which that information flows. We believe that by doing this we are giving you a powerful structure to begin developing novel ideas.

Ideas alone provide little without developing the ethic of

production, and the ability to apply that ethic towards real, useful projects. This is our second step. We want to help you develop the skills necessary to communicate knowledge in the modern context. For us, developing those skills means developing at least a basic understanding of programming, web development, media production, hardware design and statistics. We are not interested in turning you into a statistician or a programmer, what we are interested in is providing you with the resources to develop competencies in these subjects so that you can build ideas rapidly and communicate effectively with specialists you might bring on later. Like the cheap and often ad hoc home brewed experiments of the "gentlemen scientists" or the garage startups of the 1980s, we want to help you to have the abilities to rapidly tinker, share with the wider world, get appropriate feedback and develop prototypes into more sustainable projects.

Your next steps then are to use our resources first to develop ideas and then to develop the skills you'll need to put those ideas into practice and build something truly great. Good luck.

Recommended Media (Many of these books are available in audio form at Audible)

Biographies and History

Mastery by Robert Greene
Surely You Are Joking by Richard Feynman
The Information by James Gleick
The Master Switch by Tim Wu
The Ascent of Money by Niall Ferguson
Manias, Panics, Crashes by Kindleberger
A Short History of Nearly Everything by Bill Bryson

Social and Political Science

The Better Angels of Our Nature by Steven Pinker
Triumph of the City by Edward Glaeser
Situations Matter by Sam Sommers
The Social Animal by David Brooks
Social Intelligence by Daniel Goleman
Why Nations Fail by Daron Acemoglu and James Robinson
The Righteous Mind by Jonathan Haidt
The Power of Habit by Charles Duhigg
Nudge by Richard H Thaler and Cass R Sunstein

Influence by Robert Cialdini

Behavioral Economics and Irrationality

Thinking, Fast and Slow by Daniel Kaheman
Subliminal by Leonard Mlodinow
Irrationality by Stuart Sutherland
SuperSense by Bruce M. Hood
Mistakes Were Made (But Not By Me) by Carol Tavris and Elliot Aronson
Predictably Irrational by Dan Ariely
Bozo Sapiens: Why to Err is Human by Michael Kaplan and Ellen Kaplan
How We Know What Isn't So by Thomas Gilovich

Evolution and Neuroscience

Beyond Boundaries by Miguel Nicolelis
How The Mind Works by Steven Pinker
The Moral Animal by Robert Wright
On Intelligence by Jeff Hawkins
Incognito by David Eagleman
Everything is Obvious by Duncan J. Watts
The Blank Slate by Steven Pinker
How to Create a Mind by Ray Kurzweil

The Invisible Gorilla by Chistopher Chabris and Daniel Simons

Technology and the Future

Future Science by Max Brockman and Various
Physics of the Future by Michio Kaku
Alone Together by Sherry Turkle
The Rational Optimist by Matt Ridley
What Technology Wants by Kevin Kelly
Abundance by Steven Kotler and Peter H. Diamandis
The Creative Destruction of Medicine by Dr. Eric Topol
Infinite Reality by Jim Blascovich and Jeremy Bailenson
Reality Is Broken by Jane McGonigal
Information Rules by Hal Varian

Money and Finance

Economic Facts and Fallacies by Thomas Sowell
Why I Left Goldmen Sachs by Greg Smith
Reminiscences of a Stock Operator by Edwin Lefevre Finance
Liar's Poker by Michael Lewis
How Markets Fail by John Cassidy
A Random Walk Down Wall Street by Malkiel Burton
Plutocrats by Chrystia Freeland

The Big Short by Michael Lewis
All the Devils Are Here by Bethany McLean and Joe Nocera
Devil Take The Hindmost: The History of Financial Speculation by Chancellor
Intelligent Investor by Benjamin Graham

Predictions, Forecasting and Risk

Future Babble by Dan Gardner
The Black Swan by Nassim Nicholas Taleb
Antifragile by Nassim Taleb
Fooled by Randomness by Nassim Nicholas Taleb
The Signal and the Noise by Nate Silver
The Drunkard's Walk by Leonard Mlodinow
How to Lie with Statistics by Darrel Huff
How to Prove It by Daniel Velleman
Supercrunchers by Ian Ayres

Science and Skepticism

The Half-Life of Facts by Samuel Arbesman
Bad Science by Ben Goldacre
Nonsense on Stilts by Massimo Pigliucci
The Believing Brain by Michael Shermer
Denialism by Michael Specter

Philosophy

The Worldly Philosophers by Robert Heilbroner
History of Western Philosophy by Bertrand Russell
The Theory of Economic Development by Joseph Schumpeter
All Life is Problem Solving by Karl Popper
The Wealth of Nations by Adam Smith
An Enquiry Concerning Human Understanding by David Hume
Leviathan by Thomas Hobbes
The Republic by Plato
Critique of Pure Reason by Immanual Kant
Tao te Ching by Lao Tzu
The Analects by Confucius
The Will to Power by Friedrich Nietzsche

Blogs and Websites

General Knowledge

The Browser *(http://thebrowser.com/)*
Brainpickings *(http://www.brainpickings.org/)*
Quora *(http://www.quora.com/)*

Science and Technology

Edge *(http://edge.org/)*
TED *(http://www.ted.com/)*
Technology Review *(http://www.technologyreview.com/)*
Singularity Hub *(http://singularityhub.com/)*
The Society Pages *(http://thesocietypages.org/blogs/)*
Gamasutra *(http://www.gamasutra.com/php-bin/article_display.php)*

Statistics, Probability and Data

Flowing Data *(http://flowingdata.com/)*
Visualizing *(http://www.visualizing.org/)*
Freebase *(http://www.freebase.com/)*

Finance and Money

ETFdb *(http://etfdb.com/features/)*
Seeking Alpha *(http://seekingalpha.com/)*
Bankrate *(http://www.bankrate.com/)*

Behaviorial Economics and Biases

Dan Ariely *(http://danariely.com/)*
Freakonomics *(http://www.freakonomics.com/blog/)*

Recommended Media (Part II)

HTML and CSS: Design and Build Websites by Jon Duckett
HTML5 Up and Running by Mark Pilgrim
Professional JavaScript for Web Developers by Nicolas C. Zakas
Learning jQuery by Jonathan Chaffer
Programming Ruby by Andy Hunt
Agile Web Development with Rails by Sam Ruby, Dave Thomas, and David Hannson
The Art of R Programming by Norman Matloff
Arduino Cooking by Michael Margolis

Coursework

General Programming

Intro to Computer Science
(http://itunes.apple.com/us/course/intro-to-computer-science/id529181544)
Introductions to Algorithms
(http://itunes.apple.com/us/course/introduction-to-algorithms/id495066198)
Programming Methodologies
(http://itunes.apple.com/us/course/programming-methodology/id495054181)
Programming Abstractions
(http://itunes.apple.com/us/course/programming-abstractions/id495054099)

Programming Paradigms
(http://itunes.apple.com/us/course/programming-paradigms/id495054064)
Advanced Topics in Web Development
(http://itunes.apple.com/us/itunes-u/advanced-topics-in-web-development/id454017618)

Hardware and AI

Machine Learning
(http://itunes.apple.com/us/course/machine-learning/id515364596)
Applied Artificial Intelligence
(http://itunes.apple.com/us/itunes-u/applied-artificial-intelligence/id465440711)
Pre-Engineering: Intro to Micro-controllers
(http://itunes.apple.com/us/course/pre-engineering-intro-to-micro/id518401856)

Statistics, Probability and Data

Statistics 110 – Probability
(https://itunes.apple.com/us/course/statistics-110-probability/id502492375)

Tutorials

General Programming

W3 *(http://www.w3.org/community/webed/wiki/Main_Page)*
W3 School *(http://www.w3schools.com/)*
Code Academy *(http://www.codecademy.com/#!/exercises/0)*

HTML5

HTML 5 Boilerplate *(http://html5boilerplate.com/)*
HTML 5 Rocks *(http://slides.html5rocks.com/)*

CSS

Mozilla Getting Started (CSS) *(https://developer.mozilla.org/en-US/docs/CSS/Getting_Started)*

Javascript and jQuery

Net Tuts (Javascript) *(http://net.tutsplus.com/tutorials/javascript-ajax/the-best-way-to-learn-javascript/)*
jQuery First Flight *(http://www.codeschool.com/courses/jquery-air-first-flight)*

Ruby on Rails

Net Tuts (Ruby on Rails) *(http://net.tutsplus.com/tutorials/ruby/the-best-way-to-learn-ruby-on-rails/)*
Rails For Zombies *(http://www.codeschool.com/courses/rails-for-zombies-redux)*

Statistics, Probability and Data

Stats Make Me Cry *(http://www.statsmakemecry.com/)*

R

Getting Started with R
(http://scs.math.yorku.ca/index.php/R:_Getting_started_with_R)

Scilab

SciLab
(http://www.scilab.org/support/documentation/tutorials)

Arduino

Arduino Tutorials
(http://www.jeremyblum.com/category/arduino-tutorials/)

PCB Design

Open Circuits *(http://www.opencircuits.com/Main_Page)*
Fritzing *(http://mad-science.wonderhowto.com/how-to/create-practically-anything-part-1-fritzing-circuit-boards-0135002/)*

Podcasts

Algorithms and Programming

Pragmatic Podcasts
(http://itunes.apple.com/us/podcast/pragmatic-podcasts/id267255279)
Railscast *(http://itunes.apple.com/us/podcast/railscasts-mobile/id253867754)*
Learning Rails *(http://itunes.apple.com/us/podcast/learning-rails/id269213503)*

Media Production

Film Method *(http://itunes.apple.com/us/podcast/film-method/id320450292)*
2 Reel Guys *(http://itunes.apple.com/us/podcast/2reelguys/id379981652)*
The Cutting Room *(http://itunes.apple.com/us/podcast/the-cutting-room/id292530207)*
Meet the GIMP *(http://itunes.apple.com/us/podcast/meet-the-gimp/id261571629)*
Audacity to Podcast (How To) *(http://itunes.apple.com/us/podcast/audacity-to-podcast-how-to/id378425347)*

Blogs and Websites

Algorithms and Programming

Stack Overflow *(http://stackoverflow.com/)*
Net Tuts *(http://net.tutsplus.com/)*

Hardware and AI

Spark Fun *(http://www.sparkfun.com/)*
Ponoko *(https://www.ponoko.com/)*
Formulor *(http://www.formulor.de/)*
Batch PCB *(https://www.batchpcb.com/faq)*
Thingiverse *(http://www.thingiverse.com/)*

Statistics, Probability and Data

Freebase *(http://www.freebase.com/)*
Kaggle *(http://www.kaggle.com/)*

Tools and Software

Algorithms and Programming

jQuery *(http://jquery.com/)*
Ruby on Rails *(http://rubyonrails.org/)*
HTML 5 Boilerplate *(http://html5boilerplate.com/)*
YAML *(http://www.yaml.de/)*
960.gs *(http://960.gs/)*

Web Development

Amazon s3 *(http://aws.amazon.com/s3/)*
Amazon ec2 *(http://aws.amazon.com/ec2/)*
Programmable Web (APIs) *(http://www.programmableweb.com/apis/directory/1&sort=mashups)*
Google Website Toolkit *(https://developers.google.com/web-toolkit/overview)*
Wordpress *(http://wordpress.org/)*

Media Production

GIMPShop (Images) *(http://gimpshop.com/)*
Inkscape (Vectors) *(http://inkscape.org/index.php?lang=en)*
Lightworks (Film) *(http://www.lwks.com/index.php?option=com_content&view=article&id=45&Itemid=184)*
Audacity (Audio) *(http://audacity.sourceforge.net/)*

Hardware and AI

Arduino *(http://www.arduino.cc/)*
Cubify *(http://cubify.com/)*
Makerbot *(http://makerbot.com/)*
123D App *(http://www.123dapp.com/)*
My DIY CNC *(http://www.mydiycnc.com/full_product)*
KiCard PCB *(http://www.kicad-pcb.org/display/KICAD/KiCad+EDA+Software+Suite)*

Fritzing PCB *(http://fritzing.org/)*

Statistics, Probability and Data

SciLab *(http://www.scilab.org/)*
R Commander *(http://socserv.mcmaster.ca/jfox/Misc/Rcmdr/)*
R Studio Shiny *(http://www.rstudio.com/shiny/)*
Wolfram Alpha *(http://www.wolframalpha.com/)*

About the Authors

Steve Spalding is a consultant, writer, thinker, Netflix watcher, Audible listener and all around Internet-type person who is a little bit obsessed with the idea of unlocking human potential and massaging these abilities into teams of super heroes charged with saving the world.

James Gibson believes in numbers and code. He asserts that if something can't be quantified, then it doesn't exist – although he acknowledges that many things are rather hard to quantify. His friends correctly assume that, given the chance, he would probably turn himself into a robot.

www.ingramcontent.com/pod-product-compliance
Lightning Source LLC
Chambersburg PA
CBHW061517180526
45171CB00001B/213